This book belongs to

_____

Second Edition 2021

Contents

Sign of the Cross

In the name of the Father, and of the Son,
and of the Holy Spirit.
Amen.

Signum Crucis

In nomine Patris, et Filii, et Spiritus Sancti.
Amen.

The Lord's Prayer (Our Father)

Our Father, who art in heaven, hallowed be Thy name. Thy kingdom come; Thy will be done on earth as it is in heaven. Give us this day our daily bread and forgive us our trespasses as we forgive those who trespass against us. And lead us not into temptation, but deliver us from evil.
Amen.

Oratio Dominica (Pater Noster)

Pater Noster, qui es in caelis, sanctificetur nomen tuum. Adveniat regnum tuum. Fiat voluntas tua, sicut in caelo et in terra. Panem nostrum quotidianum da nobis hodie, et dimitte nobis debita nostra sicut et nos dimittimus debitoribus nostris. Et ne nos inducas in tentationem, sed libera nos a malo.
Amen.

Hail Mary

Hail Mary, full of grace, the Lord is with thee.
Blessed art thou amongst women and
blessed is the fruit of thy womb, Jesus. Holy
Mary, Mother of God, pray for us sinners,
now, and in the hour of our death.
Amen.

Ave Maria

Ave Maria, gratia plena, Dominus tecum.
Benedicta tu in mulieribus, et benedictus
fructus ventris tui, Iesus. Sancta Maria, Mater
Dei, ora pro nobis peccatoribus, nunc, et in
hora mortis nostrae.
Amen.

Doxology (Glory Be)

Glory be to the Father, and to the Son, and to the Holy Spirit. As it was in the beginning, is now, and ever shall be in the world without end.
Amen.

Doxologia

Gloria Patri, et Filio, et Spiritui Sancto. Sicut erat in principio, et nunc, et semper, et in saecula saeculorum.
Amen.

Apostles' Creed

I believe in God, the Father almighty, Creator of heaven and earth, and in Jesus Christ, His only Son, our Lord, Who was conceived by the power of the Holy Spirit and born of the Virgin Mary, suffered under Pontius Pilate, was crucified, died, and was buried; He descended into hell; on the third day He rose again from the dead; He ascended into heaven and is seated at the right hand of God, the Father Almighty; from there He will come to judge the living and the dead.
I believe in the Holy Spirit, the holy catholic Church, the communion of saints, the forgiveness of sins, the resurrection of the body, and the life everlasting.
Amen.

Symbolum Apostolorum

Credo in Deum Patrem omnipotentem, Creatorem caeli et terrae. Et in Iesum Christum, Filium eius unicum, Dominum nostrum, qui conceptus est de Spiritu Sancto, natus ex Maria Virgine, passus sub Pontio Pilato, crucifixus, mortuus, et sepultus, descendit ad inferos, tertia die resurrexit a mortuis, ascendit ad caelos, sedet ad dexteram Dei Patris omnipotentis, inde venturus est iudicare vivos et mortuos. Credo in Spiritum Sanctum, sanctam Ecclesiam catholicam, sanctorum communionem, remissionem peccatorum, carnis resurrectionem, vitam aeternam.
Amen.

Act of Contrition

O my God, I am heartily sorry for having offended You, and I detest all my sins because of Your just punishments, but most of all because they offend You, my God, who are all good and deserving of all my love. I firmly resolve, with the help of Your grace, to sin no more and avoid the near occasions of sin.
Amen.

Actus Contritionis

Deus meus, ex toto corde paenitet me
omnium meorum peccatorum, eaque
detestor, quia peccando, non solum poenas
a Te iuste statutas promeritus sum, sed
praesertim quia offendi Te, summum bonum,
ac dignum qui super omnia diligaris. Ideo
firmiter propono, adiuvante gratia Tua, de
cetero me non peccaturum peccandique
occasiones proximas fugiturum.
Amen.

Angel of God

Angel of God,
my guardian dear,
To whom His love commits me here;
Ever this [day / night] be at my side,
To light and guard, to rule and guide.
Amen.

Angele Dei

Angele Dei, qui custos es mei,
Me tibi commissum pietate superna;
[Hodie / Hac nocte] illumina, custodi, rege,
et guberna.
Amen.

Come, Holy Spirit

Come, Holy Spirit, fill the hearts of Thy faithful and kindle in them the fire of Thy love.

V. Send forth Thy Spirit and they shall be created
R. And Thou shalt renew the face of the earth.

Let us pray:
O God, Who taught the hearts of the faithful by the light of the Holy Spirit, grant that, by the gift of the same Spirit, we may be always truly wise, and ever rejoice in His consolation. Through Christ our Lord.
Amen.

Veni, Sancte Spiritus

Veni, Sancte Spiritus, reple tuorum corda fidelium, et tui amoris in eis ignem accende.

V. Emitte Spiritum tuum et creabuntur;
R. Et renovabis faciem terrae.

Oremus:
Deus, qui corda fidelium Sancti Spiritus illustratione docuisti: da nobis in eodem Spiritu recta sapere, et de eius semper consolatione gaudere. Per Christum Dominum nostrum.
Amen.

Act of Faith

O Lord God, I firmly believe each and every truth which the holy Catholic Church teaches, because Thou, O God, Who are eternal truth and wisdom which can neither deceive nor be deceived, hast revealed them all. In this faith I stand to live and die. Amen.

Act of Hope

O Lord God, through Thy grace I hope to obtain remission of all my sins and after this life eternal happiness, for Thou hast promised, Who are all powerful, faithful, kind, and merciful. In this hope I stand to live and die. Amen.

Act of Love

O Lord God, I love Thee above all things, and I love my neighbor on account of Thee, because Thou are the highest, infinite and most perfect good, worthy of all love. In this love I stand to live and die. Amen.

Actus Fidei

Domine Deus, firma fide credo et confiteor omnia et singula quae sancta ecclesia Catholica proponit, quia tu, Deus, ea omnia revelasti, qui es aeterna veritas et sapientia quae nec fallere nec falli potest. In hac fide vivere et mori statuo. Amen.

Actus Spei

Domine Deus, spero per gratiam tuam remissionem omnium peccatorum, et post hanc vitam aeternam felicitatem me esse consecuturum: quia tu promisisti, qui es infinite potens, fidelis, benignus, et misericors. In hac spe vivere et mori statuo. Amen.

Actus Caritatis

Domine Deus, amo te super omnia et proximum meum propter te, quia tu es summum, infinitum, et perfectissimum bonum, omni dilectione dignum. In hac caritate vivere et mori statuo. Amen.

Blessing Before Meals

Bless us, O Lord, and these Thy gifts which we are about to receive from Thy bounty, through Christ our Lord. Amen.

Blessing After Meals

We give Thee thanks, almighty God, for all Thy benefits, who lives and reigns for ever and ever. Amen.

V. May the Lord grant us His peace.
R. And life everlasting.
Amen.

Benedictio Ante Mensam

Benedic, Domine, nos et haec tua dona quae de tua largitate sumus sumpturi. Per Christum Dominum nostrum. Amen.

Benedictio Post Mensam

Agimus tibi gratias, omnipotens Deus, pro universis beneficiis tuis, qui vivis et regnas in saecula saeculorum. Amen.

V. Deus det nobis suam pacem.
R. Et vitam aeternam.
Amen.

The Sanctus (Holy, Holy, Holy)

Holy, holy, holy, Lord God of hosts. Heaven and earth are full of Thy glory. Hosanna in the highest. Blessed is He who comes in the name of the Lord. Hosanna in the highest.

Sanctus

Sanctus, Sanctus, Sanctus, Dominus Deus Sabaoth. Pleni sunt caeli et terra gloria tua. Hosanna in excelsis. Benedictus qui venit in nomine Domini. Hosanna in excelsis.

Te Deum

O God, we praise Thee: we acknowledge Thee to be
the Lord.
Everlasting Father, all the earth doth worship Thee.
To Thee all the Angels, the Heavens and all the
Powers,
all the Cherubim and Seraphim, unceasingly proclaim:
Holy, Holy, Holy, Lord God of Hosts!
Heaven and earth are full of the Majesty of Thy glory.
The glorious choir of the Apostles,
the wonderful company of Prophets,
the white-robed army of Martyrs, praise Thee.
Holy Church throughout the world doth acknowledge
Thee:
the Father of infinite Majesty;
Thy adorable, true and only Son;
and the Holy Spirit, the Comforter.
O Christ, Thou art the King of glory!
Thou art the everlasting Son of the Father.
Thou, having taken it upon Thyself to deliver man,
didst not disdain the Virgin's womb.
Thou overcame the sting of death and hast opened to
believers the Kingdom of Heaven.

Thou sittest at the right hand of God, in the glory of the Father.

We believe that Thou shalt come to be our Judge.

We beseech Thee, therefore, to help Thy servants whom Thou hast redeemed with Thy Precious Blood.

Make them to be numbered with Thy Saints in everlasting glory.

V. Save Thy people, O Lord, and bless Thine inheritance!

R. Govern them, and raise them up forever.

V. Every day we thank Thee.

R. And we praise Thy Name forever, yea, forever and ever.

V. O Lord, deign to keep us from sin this day.

R. Have mercy on us, O Lord, have mercy on us.

V. Let Thy mercy, O Lord, be upon us, for we have hoped in Thee.

R. O Lord, in Thee I have hoped; let me never be put to shame.

Amen.

Te Deum

Te Deum laudamus: te Dominum confitemur.
Te aeternum Patrem omnis terra veneratur.
Tibi omnes Angeli; tibi Caeli et universae Potestates;
Tibi Cherubim et Seraphim incessabili voce
proclamant:
Sanctus, Sanctus, Sanctus, Dominus Deus Sabaoth.
Pleni sunt caeli et terra maiestatis gloriae tuae.
Te gloriosus Apostolorum chorus,
Te Prophetarum laudabilis numerus,
Te Martyrum candidatus laudat exercitus.
Te per orbem terrarum sancta confitetur Ecclesia,
Patrem immensae maiestatis:
Venerandum tuum verum et unicum Filium;
Sanctum quoque Paraclitum Spiritum.
Tu Rex gloriae, Christe.
Tu Patris sempiternus es Filius.
Tu ad liberandum suscepturus hominem, non
horruisti Virginis uterum.
Tu, devicto mortis aculeo, aperuisti credentibus regna
caelorum.

Tu ad dexteram Dei sedes, in gloria Patris.
Iudex crederis esse venturus.
Te ergo quaesumus, tuis famulis subveni: quos
pretioso sanguine redemisti.
Aeterna fac cum sanctis tuis in gloria numerari.

V. Salvum fac populum tuum, Domine, et benedic
hereditati tuae.
R. Et rege eos, et extolle illos usque in aeternum.
V. Per singulos dies benedicimus te.
R. Et laudamus nomen tuum in saeculum, et in
saeculum saeculi.
V. Dignare, Domine, die isto sine peccato nos
custodire.
R. Miserere nostri, Domine, miserere nostri.
V. Fiat misericordia tua, Domine, super nos,
quemadmodum speravimus in te.
R. In te, Domine, speravi: non confundar in aeternum.
Amen.

We Adore Thee

We adore Thee, most holy Lord Jesus Christ, here and in all Thy churches that are in the whole world, and we bless Thee; because by Thy Holy Cross Thou hast redeemed the World.
Amen.

Adoremus Te

Adoremus te, sanctissime Domine Iesu Christe, hic et ad omnes Ecclesias tuas, quae sunt in toto mundo, et benedicimus tibi; quia per sanctam Crucem tuam redemisti mundum.
Amen.

Prayer Before a Crucifix

O most high, glorious God, illuminate the darkness of my heart. Grant me, O Lord, a right faith, certain hope, and a perfect charity, sense and knowledge that I may carry out Thy Holy and true command.
Amen.

Oratio ante crucifixum

Summe, gloriose Deus, illumina tenebras
cordis mei, et da mihi fidem rectam, spem
certam et caritatem perfectam, sensum et
cognitionem, Domine, ut faciam tuum
sanctum et verax mandatum.
Amen.

Lord Jesus Christ, Son of the Loving God
(Prayer after Mass)

O Lord Jesus Christ, Son of the living God, who from the will of the Father, with the cooperation of the Holy Spirit, hast by Thy death given life unto the world, deliver me by Thy most sacred Body, which, I, unworthy, have presumed to receive, from all my iniquities and from every evil, and make me ever to hold fast to Thy commandments and suffer me never to be separated from Thee. Amen.

Domine Iesu Christe

Domine Iesu Christe, Fili Dei vivi, qui ex
voluntate Patris, cooperante Spiritu Sancto,
per mortem tuam mundum vivificasti, libera
me per sacrosanctum Corpus tuum, quod
ego indignus sumere praesumpsi, ab
omnibus iniquitatibus meis et universis malis,
et fac me tuis semper inhaerere mandatis et
a te numquam separari permittas.
Amen.

Soul of Christ

Soul of Christ, sanctify me.
Body of Christ, save me.
Blood of Christ, inebriate me.
Water from the side of Christ, wash me.
Passion of Christ, strengthen me.
O good Jesus, hear me.
Within Thy wounds, hide me.
Separated from Thee let me never be.
From the malignant enemy, defend me.
At the hour of death, call me.
To come to Thee, bid me,
That I may praise Thee in the company
Of Thy Saints, for all eternity.
Amen.

Anima Christi

Anima Christi, sanctifica me.
Corpus Christi, salva me.
Sanguis Christi, inebria me.
Aqua lateris Christi, lava me.
Passio Christi, conforta me.
O bone Iesu, exaudi me.
Intra tua vulnera absconde me.
Ne permittas me separari a te.
Ab hoste maligno defende me.
In hora mortis meae voca me.
Et iube me venire ad te,
Ut cum Sanctis tuis laudem te
in saecula saeculorum.
Amen.

O Saving Victim

O Saving Victim opening wide
The gate of heaven to all below.
Our foes press on from every side;
Thine aid supply, Thy strength bestow.

To Thy great name be endless praise
Immortal Godhead, One in Three;
Oh, grant us endless length of days,
In our true native land with Thee.

O Salutaris Hostia

O Salutaris Hostia
Quae caeli pandis ostium.
Bella premunt hostilia;
Da robur, fer auxilium.

Uni trinoque Domino
Sit sempiterna gloria:
Qui vitam sine termino,
Nobis donet in patria.

Amen.

Down in Adoration Falling

Down in adoration falling,
Lo! the sacred Host we hail,
Lo! oe'r ancient forms departing
Newer rites of grace prevail;
Faith for all defects supplying,
Where the feeble senses fail.

To the everlasting Father,
And the Son Who reigns on high
With the Holy Spirit proceeding
Forth from each eternally,
Be salvation, honor blessing,
Might and endless majesty.

Amen.

Tantum Ergo

Tantum ergo Sacramentum
Veneremur cernui:
Et antiquum documentum
Novo cedat ritui:
Praestet fides supplementum
Sensuum defectui.

Genitori, Genitoque
Laus et iubilatio,
Salus, honor, virtus quoque
Sit et benedictio:
Procedenti ab utroque
Compar sit laudatio.

Amen.

Divine Praises

Blessed be God.
Blessed be His Holy Name.
Blessed be Jesus Christ, true God and true man.
Blessed be the name of Jesus.
Blessed be His Most Sacred Heart.
Blessed be His Most Precious Blood.
Blessed be Jesus in the Most Holy Sacrament of the Altar.
Blessed be the Holy Spirit the Paraclete.
Blessed be the great Mother of God, Mary Most Holy.
Blessed be her holy and Immaculate Conception.
Blessed be her glorious Assumption.
Blessed be the name of Mary, Virgin and Mother.
Blessed be St. Joseph, her most chaste spouse.
Blessed be God in His Angels and in His Saints.
Amen.

Laudes Divinae

Benedictus Deus.
Benedictum Nomen Sanctum eius.
Benedictus Iesus Christus, verus Deus et verus homo.
Benedictum Nomen Iesu.
Benedictum Cor eius sacratissimum.
Benedictus Sanguis eius pretiosissimus.
Benedictus Iesus in sanctissimo altaris Sacramento.
Benedictus Sanctus Spiritus, Paraclitus.
Benedicta excelsa Mater Dei, Maria sanctissima.
Benedicta sancta eius et immaculata Conceptio.
Benedicta eius gloriosa Assumptio.
Benedictum nomen Mariae, Virginis et Matris.
Benedictus sanctus Ioseph, eius castissimus Sponsus.
Benedictus Deus in Angelis suis, et in Sanctis suis.
Amen.

Hidden God, I Adore Thee

Godhead here in hiding, whom I do adore,
Masked by these bare shadows, shape and
nothing more,
See, Lord, at your service low lies here a heart
Lost, all lost in wonder at the God you are.

Seeing, touching, tasting are in thee deceived:
How says trusty hearing? that shall be believed;
What God's Son has told me, take for truth I do;
Truth Himself speaks truly or there's nothing
true.

On the cross your godhead made no sign to men,
Here your very manhood steals from human ken:
Both are my confession, both are my belief,
And I pray the prayer of the dying thief.

I am not like Thomas, wounds I cannot see,
But can plainly call you Lord and God as he;
Let me to a deeper faith daily nearer move,
Daily make me harder hope and dearer love.

You are our reminder of Christ crucified,
Living Bread, the life of us for whom he died,
Lend this life to me then: feed and feast my mind
With your sweetness that we all were meant to
find.

Bring the tender tale true of the Pelican;
Bathe me, Jesu Lord, in what your bosom ran
Blood whereof a single drop has power to win
All the world forgiveness of its world of sin.

Jesu, whom I look at shrouded here below,
I beseech you send me what I thirst for so,
Some day to gaze on you face to face in light
And be blest for ever with your glory's sight.
Amen.

Adoro Te Devote

Adoro deuote, latens ueritas,
te que sub his formis uere latitas.
Tibi se cor meum totum subicit,
quia te contemplans totum deficit.

Visus, tactus, gustus in te fallitur,
sed auditu solo tute creditur.
Credo quicquid dixit dei filius,
nichil ueritatis uerbo uerius.

In cruce latebat sola deitas,
sed hic latet simul et humanitas.
Ambo uere credens atque confitens,
peto quod petiuit latro penitens

.

Plagas sicut Thomas non intueor,
deum tamen meum te confiteor.
Fac me tibi semper magis credere,
in te spem habere, te diligere.

O memoriale mortis domini,
panis uiuus uitam prestans homini.
Presta michi semper de te uiuere,
et te michi semper dulce sapere.

Pie pellicane, Ihesu domine,
me immundum munda tuo sanguine.
Cuius una stilla saluum facere,
totum mundum posset omni scelere.

Ihesu, quem uelatum nunc aspicio,
quando fiet illud quod tam sicio?
te reuelata cernens facie,
uisu sim beatus tue glorie.

Canticle of Mary (Magnificat)

My soul doth magnify the Lord,
and my spirit hath rejoiced in God my Savior.
For He hath regarded the humility of His handmaiden.
For behold, from henceforth all generations shall call
me blessed.

For He that is mighty hath done great things to me,
and holy is His Name.
And His Mercy is from generation unto generations
upon them that fear Him.

He hath shewed might in His arm,
He hath scattered the proud in the conceit of their
heart.
He hath put down the mighty from their seat,
and hath exalted the humble.
He hath filled the hungry with good things,
and the rich He hath sent empty away.

He hath received Israel, His servant,
being mindful of His mercy.
As He spoke to our Fathers,
Abraham and his seed forever.

Magnificat

Magnificat anima mea Dominum,
et exultavit spiritus meus in Deo salvatore meo,
quia respexit humilitatem ancillae suae.
Ecce enim ex hoc beatam me dicent omnes
generationes,

quia fecit mihi magna, qui potens est.
et sanctum nomen eius,
et misericordia eius in progenies et progenies
timentibus eum.

Fecit potentiam in brachio suo,
dispersit superbos mente cordi sui;
deposuit potentes de sede
et exaltavit humiles;
esurientes implevit bonis
et divites dimisit inanes.

Suscepit Israel puerum suum,
recordatus misericordiae,
sicut locutus est ad patres nostros,
Abraham et semini eius in saecula.

The Memorare

Remember, O most gracious Virgin Mary, that never was it known that anyone who fled to thy protection, implored thy help, or sought thy intercession was left unaided. Inspired with this confidence, I fly to thee, O Virgin of virgins, my Mother; to thee do I come; before thee I stand, sinful and sorrowful. O Mother of the Word Incarnate, despise not my petitions, but in thy mercy hear and answer me.
Amen.

Memorare, O piissima Virgo Maria

Memorare, O piissima Virgo Maria, non esse auditum a saeculo, quemquam ad tua currentem praesidia, tua implorantem auxilia, tua petentem suffragia, esse derelictum. Ego tali animatus confidentia, ad te, Virgo Virginum, Mater, curro, ad te venio, coram te gemens peccator assisto. Noli, Mater Verbi, verba mea despicere; sed audi propitia et exaudi.
Amen.

Queen of Heaven

O Queen of heaven rejoice! alleluia:
For He whom thou didst merit to bear,
alleluia,
Hath arisen as he said, alleluia.
Pray for us to God, alleluia.
Rejoice and be glad, O Virgin Mary, alleluia.
Because the Lord is truly risen, alleluia.

O God, who gave joy to the world through
the resurrection of Thy Son, our Lord Jesus
Christ, grant we beseech Thee, that through
the intercession of the Virgin Mary, His
Mother, we may obtain the joys of everlasting
life. Through the same Christ our Lord.
Amen.

Regina Caeli

Regina, caeli, laetare, alleluia:
Quia quem meruisti portare, alleluia,
Resurrexit sicut dixit, alleluia.
Ora pro nobis Deum, alleluia.
Gaude et laetare, Virgo Maria, alleluia,
Quia surrexit Dominus vere, alleluia.

Deus, qui per resurrectionem Filii tui, Domini
nostri Iesu Christi, mundum laetificare
dignatus es: praesta, quaesumus; ut per eius
Genetricem Virginem Mariam, perpetuae
capiamus gaudia vitae. Per eundem Christum
Dominum nostrum.
Amen

Hail Holy Queen

Hail Holy Queen, Mother of mercy, our life, our sweetness, and our hope. To thee do we cry, poor banished children of Eve. To thee do we send up our sighs, mourning and weeping in this valley of tears.
Turn then, most gracious Advocate, thine eyes of mercy toward us. And after this our exile show unto us the blessed fruit of thy womb, Jesus.
O clement, O loving, O sweet Virgin Mary.

V. Pray for us, O Holy Mother of God.
R. That we may be made worthy of the promises of Christ.
Amen

Salve Regina

Salve, Regina, mater misericordiae, vita, dulcedo, et spes nostra, salve. Ad te clamamus exsules filii Hevae. Ad te suspiramus, gementes et flentes in hac lacrimarum valle.
Eia, ergo, advocata nostra, illos tuos misericordes oculos ad nos converte. Et Iesum, benedictum fructum ventris tui, nobis post hoc exsilium ostende.
O clemens, O pia, O dulcis Virgo Maria.

V. Ora pro nobis, sancta Dei Genetrix.
R. Ut digni efficiamur promissionibus Christi.
Amen.

Hail Star of the Sea

Hail, O Star of the sea,
God's own Mother blest,
ever sinless Virgin,
gate of heavenly rest.

Taking that sweet Ave,
which from Gabriel came,
peace confirm within us,
changing Eve's name.

Break the sinners' fetters,
make our blindness day,
Chase all evils from us,
for all blessings pray.

Show thyself a Mother,
may the Word divine
born for us thine Infant
hear our prayers through thine.

Virgin all excelling,
mildest of the mild,
free from guilt preserve us
meek and undefiled.

Keep our life all spotless,
make our way secure
till we find in Jesus,
joy for evermore.

Praise to God the Father,
honor to the Son,
in the Holy Spirit,
be the glory one.
Amen.

Ave Maris Stella

Ave maris stella,
Dei Mater alma,
atque semper Virgo,
felix caeli porta.

Sumens illud Ave
Gabrielis ore,
funda nos in pace,
mutans Hevae nomen.

Solve vincula reis,
profer lumen caecis
mala nostra pelle,
bona cuncta posce.

Monstra te esse matrem:
sumat per te preces,
qui pro nobis natus,
tulit esse tuus.

Virgo singularis,
inter omnes mites,
nos culpis solutos,
mitis fac et castos.

Vitam praesta puram,
iter para tutum:
ut videntes Iesum
semper collaetemur.

Sit laus Deo Patri,
summo Christo decus,
Spiritui Sancto,
tribus honor unus.
Amen.

Prayer to St. Michael

Saint Michael the Archangel, defend us in battle; be our defense against the wickedness and snares of the devil. May God rebuke him, we humbly pray. And do thou, O prince of the heavenly host, by the power of God thrust into hell Satan and all the evil spirits who prowl about the world for the ruin of souls.
Amen.

Oratio ad Sanctum Michael

Sancte Michael Archangele, defende nos in proelio, contra nequitiam et insidias diaboli esto praesidium. Imperet illi Deus, supplices deprecamur: tuque, Princeps militiae caelestis, Satanam aliosque spiritus malignos, qui ad perditionem animarum pervagantur in mundo, divina virtute, in infernum detrude. Amen.

Prayer Intentions

Prayer Intentions

Prayer Intentions

Prayer Intentions

Prayer Intentions

Prayer Intentions

Prayer Intentions

Prayer Intentions

Prayer Intentions

Made in the USA
Las Vegas, NV
03 November 2023

80060530R00039